Reproducible Forms

for the Writing Traits Classroom: **K-2**

Ruth Culham

New York • Toronto • London • Auckland • Sydney
Mexico City • New Delhi • Hong Kong • Buenos Aires

Teaching *Resources*

Dedication

For Joseph, Ted, Mallery, Allen, and Samantha

Cover design by Maria Lilja
Interior design by Sarah Morrow

Copyright © 2006 by Ruth Culham
All rights reserved. Published by Scholastic Inc.
Printed in the U.S.A.
ISBN-10: 0-439-82133-9
ISBN-13: 978-0-439-82133-9

2 3 4 5 6 7 8 9 10   40   12 11 10 09 08 07 06

Contents

Introduction

Teachers are the ultimate multitaskers in the world, but rarely do they have the time to create all the materials and forms they know would streamline planning and classroom management. This is especially true when it comes to teaching young students how to write. That's where this book can help. The forms provided here are designed to simplify many teaching processes: They will help you identify and document strengths and needs of individual students, monitor their progress, plan writing instruction, communicate with parents, and keep track of it all as simply as possible. In addition, there are forms to support your students as they develop as writers.

These forms have their origins in classrooms just like yours. Over the years, I've collected, tested, and adapted forms that make teaching easier, and here I present the best of the best for primary writing traits teachers. I hope they serve you well, freeing up time you can devote to the most important job of all— teaching young students.

This book is divided into two parts. Part one contains forms for you, the teacher, to use as you assess and provide writing instruction to primary students.

Part two contains forms that students will find ready to use and apply to their writing as it develops. This book can be used on its own or as a companion to *6+1 Traits of Writing: The Complete Guide for the Primary Grades* (Scholastic, 2005). And since the pages are full-size blackline masters, you'll be able to easily choose which forms you want to use and when. Just photocopy your choices and you'll be ready to try them with individuals, small groups, or your whole class. In this book you'll find forms including:

* scoring guides written just for K–2 students

* feedback forms designed for use by K–2 students

* record-keeping forms

* lesson planning templates

* parent letters

* trait songs

* graphic organizers for each trait

* and more

Some Background on the Traits

The traits of writing drive classroom talk. They provide the language we use to describe what writers really do as they draft, revise, and edit. Introducing this language right from the start helps primary students see themselves as writers and lays a strong foundation for future work. I discuss teaching writing with the traits in depth in *6+1 Traits of Writing*; here is an overview of the traits and how they are manifested in the youngest writers.

(IDEAS) *the meaning and development of the message*

Signs of the ideas trait in primary writing/drawing:

* Complexity in color, shape, and lines

* Attention to details

* A topic that is narrow enough to handle

* Noticing things others might not notice

* Clarity, focus, and sense of purpose

* A message or story, complete or not

(ORGANIZATION) *the internal structure of the piece*

Signs of the organization trait in primary writing/drawing:

* Pictures and/or text balanced on the page
* Coordination between text and pictures
* Grouping of details
* Use of sequence words: first, then, after, next, later, last
* Sense of beginning: one day, last week, when I was little
* Sense of ending: at last, that's all, the end
* Cause and effect, problem solving, chronological sequence in pictures and text

(VOICE) *the way the writer brings the topic to life*

Signs of the voice trait in primary writing/drawing:

* Individuality and sparkle
* Liveliness, playfulness with the topic
* The unusual; trying something new
* Recognizing audience
* A sense of what the writer thinks and feels

(WORD CHOICE) *the specific vocabulary the writer uses to convey meaning*

Signs of the word choice trait in primary writing/drawing:

* Playing with and imitating letter and word forms
* Stretching to use new words
* Verbs that have energy
* Precise words
* Unusual use of words or phrases
* Striking or memorable words or phrases

SENTENCE FLUENCY — *the way the words and phrases flow throughout the text*

Signs of the sentence fluency trait in primary writing/drawing:

* Experimenting with word strings to form sentences
* Simple sentences
* Rhythm and cadence, phrasing
* Long and short sentences
* Sentences that begin differently
* Using rhythmic language (poetry)

CONVENTIONS — *the mechanical correctness of the piece*

Signs of the conventions trait in primary writing/drawing:

* Left to right, up to down orientation on the page
* Distinction between upper- and lowercase letters
* Spaces between words
* Capital letters at the beginning of sentences and on the pronoun *I*.
* Use of punctuation at the end of sentences
* Correct spelling for the age; readable on other words

PRESENTATION — *the overall appearance of the work*

Signs of the presentation trait in primary writing/drawing:

* Neatness
* Letters and words on the lines
* Careful handwriting
* Nicely drawn pictures
* Use of margins
* No smudges or cross-outs

Primary writers need time and guidance to develop the writing skills necessary to create text that expresses their ideas in unique and individual ways. Learning about the traits and applying them to their writing in a systematic way that is reinforced each year gives them the language and specific tools needed to become good writers—great writers. Use the forms in this book to help you with this important work. I'm excited to share them with you and hope they are a welcome addition to your trait-based resource collection.

Reproducible Writing Traits Forms for Teachers

It's never too early to begin using the traits of writing to encourage your young students as they become skilled and confident writers. From the time that primary students begin to capture their ideas in pictures and early representations of letters and words, to the point that they are writing fully developed paragraphs with multiple sentences on the same topic, the traits can provide much-needed and appreciated writing support. In schools where students, teachers, administrators, and even parents use trait language to talk about and celebrate writing, growth is measurable and improvement is sustainable. Conversations among students, teachers, and parents can center on the traits, and students begin to embrace them as central to their understanding of how writing works.

First and foremost, the traits of writing are a powerful assessment tool. Each of the traits—ideas, organization, voice, word choice, sentence fluency, conventions, and presentation—has a detailed and user-friendly scoring guide that helps teachers determine where students are in their development as writers. From this information, thoughtful instructional lesson plans can be created that support students as they move from one developmental level of the scoring guide to the next.

The first part of this book is dedicated to forms that teachers will find useful in the trait-based writing classroom. It is divided into three sections:

* Rubrics and Assessment Feedback Help

* Record-Keeping and Planning Forms

* Parent Communication

Designed for the busy and time-conscious teacher, these forms support the primary classroom where the traits are used as tools to assess and communicate to students and families about writing progress. It's exciting for teachers to be able to document growth with such accuracy and specificity, and the forms here will help you do so with ease.

Rubrics and Assessment Feedback Help

Use the scoring guides provided in this section as well as the other forms designed to help you assess and respond to student writing as you begin working with the traits.

Primary Writing Assessment Scoring Guides

The scoring guides for each trait are used to assess student writing. Each guide describes characteristics of writing within a trait, simplifying the process of matching student performance to a level of writing proficiency, from "Ready to Begin" to "Established." You can choose to assess for all the traits, or one, or more, depending on what has been taught and what your goals for the writing might be.

These scoring guides are the foundation of all trait-based work that takes place in the primary classroom. They are used to assess writing; they provide the common language for talking about writing; and they are the core elements of the mini-lessons for writing workshop.

The holistic scoring guide captures the progression of writing skills typically exhibited by primary writers. You can use it to assess the writing as a whole, the sum of its parts.

(Note: Reproducible scoring guides taken from *6+1 Traits of Writing: The Complete Guide for the Primary Grades,* Scholastic, 2005.*)*

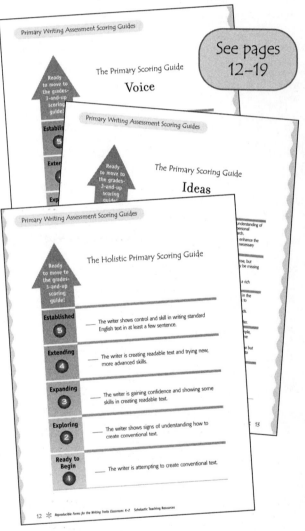

Paper Clipper Scores

Cut apart these Paper Clippers and attach one to a student's piece to let her know the result of your assessment in one or more of the traits. You can highlight the area you want students to work on most by circling or highlighting the trait or traits for revision or further editing.

Minh	5	4	3	2	1
Ideas		✓			
Organization			✓		
Voice			✓		
Word Choice			✓		
Sentence Fluency				✓	
Conventions			✓		
Presentation			✓		

See page 20

Student Feedback Forms

The Student Feedback Forms allow you to focus in on one trait at a time as you respond to students' work. By using the continuum, you can show students how close to "Strong" their paper is in that trait. You can provide a suggestion or two to make the piece even better in the comment section.

Name _Maria Muñoz_   Date _March 16_

Paper title _My Cat Bailey_

Ideas: the main message

See how strong your idea is and how to make it better.

1 — Beginning (on your mark)   3 — Developing (get set)   5 — Strong (go!)

Here is a suggestion for revision: _Try adding two more details of things Bailey does that makes her a "funny cat."_

See pages 21–24

The Holistic Primary Scoring Guide

Ready to move to the grades-3-and-up scoring guide!

Established

5

_____ The writer shows control and skill in writing standard English text in at least a few sentence.s

Extending

4

_____ The writer is creating readable text and trying new, more advanced skills.

Expanding

3

_____ The writer is gaining confidence and showing some skills in creating readable text.

Exploring

2

_____ The writer shows signs of understanding how to create conventional text.

Ready to Begin

1

_____ The writer is attempting to create conventional text.

The Primary Scoring Guide

Ideas

Ready to move to the grades-3-and-up scoring guide!

Established (5)

____ The idea is clear and coherent.

____ The text is a well-developed paragraph.

____ Elaboration through interesting details creates meaning for the reader.

____ The writer shows understanding of the topic through personal experience or research.

____ Pictures (if present) enhance the key ideas but aren't necessary for comprehension.

Extending (4)

____ The writing works by itself to explain a simple idea or story.

____ The writing is made up of several sentences on one topic.

____ Key details begin to surface.

____ The writing makes sense, but some information may be missing or irrelevant.

____ Pictures and text work harmoniously to create a rich treatment of the topic.

Expanding (3)

____ The idea is written in a basic sentence.

____ A simple statement with somewhat detailed pictures captures the topic.

____ Basic details are present in the text; the illustrations work to enhance the main idea.

____ The text contains real words.

____ Text and picture are understandable to the reader.

Exploring (2)

____ One or more ideas are present in the most general way.

____ Letters and words can be picked out as clues to the topic.

____ The drawing helps to clarify the idea.

____ The text is composed of simple, recognizable letters with some early attempts at words.

____ The reader gets the basic idea but needs the writer's assistance to comprehend it fully.

Ready to Begin (1)

____ The piece conveys little meaning.

____ Real-life objects show up in drawings.

____ Drawings may not be completely recognizable.

____ Letters are not consistent or standard.

____ An oral reading by the writer is needed to understand the message.

Ready to move to the grades-3-and-up scoring guide!

The Primary Scoring Guide

Organization

Established 5

____ The title (if present) is thoughtful and effective.

____ There is a clear beginning, middle, and end.

____ Important ideas are highlighted within the text.

____ Everything fits together nicely.

____ The text slows down and speeds up to highlight the ideas and shows the writer's skill at pacing.

____ Clear transitions connect one sentence to the next.

Extending 4

____ The title (if present) comes close to capturing the central idea.

____ The writing starts out strong and includes a predictable ending.

____ The writer uses a pattern to spotlight the most important details.

____ Ideas follow a logical but obvious sequence.

____ The writing's pace is even; it doesn't bog the reader down.

____ Basic transitions link one sentence to the next.

Expanding 3

____ The simple title (if present) states the topic.

____ The piece contains a beginning but not a conclusion.

____ The piece is little more than a list of sentences connected by a theme.

____ There is basic order with a few missteps.

____ There is more text at the beginning than in the middle or end.

____ Sentence parts are linked with conjunctions (but, and, or).

Exploring 2

____ The piece has no title.

____ Letters or words are used as captions.

____ Simple clues about order emerge in pictures or text.

____ No transitions are indicated.

____ The arrangement of pictures or text shows an awareness of the importance of structure and pattern.

____ Left-to-right, top-to-bottom orientation is evident.

Ready to Begin 1

____ Letters (if present) are scattered across the page.

____ No coordination of written elements is evident.

____ Lines, pictures, or letters are randomly placed on the page.

____ Lines, pictures, or letters are grouped haphazardly.

____ There is no sense of order.

The Primary Scoring Guide

Voice

Ready to move to the grades-3-and-up scoring guide!

Established
5

- ____ The writer "owns" the topic.
- ____ The piece contains the writer's imprint.
- ____ The writer is mindful of the piece's audience and connects purposefully with the reader.
- ____ The tone is identifiable—bittersweet, compassionate, frustrated, terrified, and so on.
- ____ The writer takes real risks, creating a truly individual piece of writing.

Extending
4

- ____ The writer takes a standard topic and addresses it in a nonstandard way.
- ____ The writer tries a new word, interesting image, or unusual detail.
- ____ The writing speaks to the reader in several places.
- ____ The writing captures a general mood such as happy, sad, or mad.
- ____ The writer begins to show how he or she really thinks and feels about the topic.

Expanding
3

- ____ There are fleeting glimpses of how the writer looks at the topic.
- ____ Touches of originality are found in the text and pictures.
- ____ There is a moment of audience awareness, but then it fades.
- ____ BIG letters, exclamation points, underlining, repetition, and pictures are used for emphasis.
- ____ A pat summary statement conceals the writer's individuality.

Exploring
2

- ____ The piece is a routine response to the assignment.
- ____ The writer copies environmental text but also adds an original bit.
- ____ The text connects with the reader in the most general way.
- ____ The drawings begin to reveal the individual.
- ____ The barest hint of the writer is in evidence.

Ready to Begin
1

- ____ The reader is not sure why the writer chose this idea for writing.
- ____ The writer tries to copy without purpose what he or she sees around the room.
- ____ No awareness of audience is evident.
- ____ The piece contains very simple drawings or lines.
- ____ Nothing distinguishes the work to make it the writer's own.

The Primary Scoring Guide

Word Choice

Ready to move to the grades-3-and-up scoring guide!

Established
5

____ The writer uses everyday words and phrases with a fresh and original spin.

____ The words paint a clear picture in the reader's mind.

____ The writer uses just the right words or phrase.

____ Figurative language works reasonably well.

____ Colorful words are used correctly and with creativity.

Extending
4

____ Descriptive nouns (e.g., Raisin Bran, not cereal) are combined with generic ones.

____ The writer uses an active verb or two.

____ There is very little repetition of words.

____ The writer attempts figurative language.

____ The writer "stretches" by using different types of words.

Expanding
3

____ Some words make sense.

____ The reader begins to see what the writer is describing.

____ One or two words stand out.

____ Occasional misuse of words bogs the reader down.

____ The writer tries out new words.

Exploring
2

____ Conventional letters are present.

____ The letter strings begin to form words.

____ Letter strings can be read as words even though the spacing and spelling isn't correct.

____ Words from the board, displays, or word walls are attempted.

____ A few words can be identified.

Ready to Begin
1

____ Scribbling and random lines mark the page.

____ Imitation letters may be present.

____ There may be random strings of letters across the page.

____ Writer uses his or her name.

____ Few, if any, recognizable words are present.

The Primary Scoring Guide

Sentence Fluency

Ready to move to the grades-3-and-up scoring guide!

Established 5

____ Different sentence lengths give the writing a nice sound. There is playfulness and experimentation.

____ Varied sentence beginnings create a pleasing rhythm.

____ The piece is a breeze to read aloud.

____ Different kinds of sentences (statements, commands, questions, and exclamations) are present.

____ The flow from one sentence to the next is smooth.

Extending 4

____ Sentences are of different lengths.

____ Sentences start differently.

____ Some sentences read smoothly while others still need work.

____ Connectives are correctly used in long and short sentences.

____ Aside from a couple of awkward moments, the piece can be read aloud easily.

Expanding 3

____ Basic subject-verb agreement occurs in simple sentences— e.g., "I jumped."

____ Sentence beginnings are identical, making all sentences sound alike.

____ Longer sentences go on and on.

____ Simple conjunctions such as *and* and *but* are used to make compound sentences.

____ The piece is easy to read aloud, although it may contain repetitive or awkward sentence patterns.

Exploring 2

____ Written elements work together in units.

____ Words are combined to make short, repetitive phrases.

____ Awkward word patterns break the flow of the piece.

____ The reader gets only one or two clues about how the pictures and text are connected.

____ The writer stumbles when reading the text aloud and may have to back up and reread.

Ready to Begin 1

____ It's hard to figure out how the elements go together.

____ Words, if present, stand alone.

____ Imitation words and letters are used across the page.

____ There is no overall sense of flow to the piece.

____ Only the writer can read the piece aloud.

Ready to move to the grades-3-and-up scoring guide!

The Primary Scoring Guide

Conventions

Established

5

____ High-use words are spelled correctly and others are easy to read.

____ The writer applies basic capitalization rules with consistency.

____ Punctuation marks are used effectively to guide the reader.

____ One or more paragraphs with indenting are present.

____ Standard English grammar is used.

____ Conventions are applied consistently and correctly.

Extending

4

____ Spelling is correct or close on high-use words (*kiten, saed, want*).

____ Sentence beginnings and proper nouns are usually capitalized.

____ The writer uses end punctuation and series commas correctly.

____ The writer may try more advanced punctuation (dashes, ellipses, quotation marks) but not always with success.

____ Only minor editing is required to show thoughtful use of conventions.

Expanding

3

____ Spelling is inconsistent (phonetic spelling—e.g., *kitn, sed, wtn*) but readable.

____ Upper- and lowercase letters are used correctly.

____ Capitals mark the beginning of sentences.

____ End punctuation marks are generally used correctly.

____ The writing correctly follows simple conventions.

Exploring

2

____ The words are unreadable to the untrained eye (quasi-phonetic spelling—e.g., *KN, sD, Wt*).

____ There is little discrimination between upper- and lowercase letters.

____ Spacing between letters and words is present.

____ The writer experiments with punctuation.

____ The use of conventions is not consistent.

Ready to Begin

1

____ Letters are written in strings (pre-phonetic spelling—e.g., *gGmkrRt*).

____ Letters are formed irregularly; there is no intentional use of upper- and lowercase letters.

____ Spacing is uneven between letters and words.

____ Punctuation is not present.

____ The piece does not employ standard conventions.

The Primary Scoring Guide

Presentation

Ready to move to the grades-3-and-up scoring guide!

Established 5

____ The margins frame the text for easy reading.

____ Pictures and text look planned and work where they are placed.

____ The handwriting is legible and consistent in form.

____ There are no stray marks, cross-outs, or tears on the paper.

____ The overall appearance is neat and pleasing to the eye.

Extending 4

____ Margins are present but not consistent.

____ White space is used effectively, but words or pictures are often jammed at the end of lines.

____ Most letters are formed correctly and legibly.

____ A few cross-outs and smudges mar an otherwise pleasing appearance.

____ The overall presentation is organized with only minor distractions.

Expanding 3

____ Margins show awareness of left-to-right/top-to-bottom directionality, though they are not evenly spaced.

____ White space is present but inconsistent in size.

____ The handwriting is more legible at the beginning than at the end.

____ There are cross-outs and stray marks but only a few small smudges or tears from erasing.

____ The piece looks rushed.

Exploring 2

____ Attempts at margins are inconsistent.

____ The writing contains irregular chunks of white space.

____ Letters slant in different directions and form different shapes and sizes.

____ Many cross-outs, marks, and tears divert attention.

____ Only a last-minute attempt was made to create a readable piece.

Ready to Begin 1

____ No margins are present.

____ The use of white space is random and ineffective.

____ The handwriting is messy and illegible.

____ There are many cross-outs, stray marks, or tears from erasing.

____ Little care went into this piece to make it readable or understandable.

Paper Clipper Scores

	5	4	3	2	1
Ideas					
Organization					
Voice					
Word Choice					
Sentence Fluency					
Conventions					
Presentation					

	5	4	3	2	1
Ideas					
Organization					
Voice					
Word Choice					
Sentence Fluency					
Conventions					
Presentation					

	5	4	3	2	1
Ideas					
Organization					
Voice					
Word Choice					
Sentence Fluency					
Conventions					
Presentation					

	5	4	3	2	1
Ideas					
Organization					
Voice					
Word Choice					
Sentence Fluency					
Conventions					
Presentation					

Name_____ Date_____

Paper title_____

Ideas: the main message

See how strong your idea is and how to make it better.

```
        1                    3                    5
  •─────•────────────────────•────────────────────•──────────────>
     Beginning            Developing            Strong
   (on your mark)         (get set)             (go!)
```

Here is a suggestion for revision:

Name_____ Date_____

Paper title_____

Organization: the order and structure

See how strong your organization is and how to make it better.

```
        1                    3                    5
  •─────•────────────────────•────────────────────•──────────────>
     Beginning            Developing            Strong
   (on your mark)         (get set)             (go!)
```

Here is a suggestion for revision:

Name_____ Date_____

Paper title_____

Voice: my personal style

See how strong your voice is and how to make it better.

```
        1                    3                    5
   •────●────────────────────●────────────────────●──────────▶
     Beginning            Developing            Strong
   (on your mark)         (get set)             (go!)
```

Here is a suggestion for revision:

Name_____ Date_____

Paper title_____

Word Choice: colorful and interesting words

See how strong your word choice is and how to make it better.

```
        1                    3                    5
   •────●────────────────────●────────────────────●──────────▶
     Beginning            Developing            Strong
   (on your mark)         (get set)             (go!)
```

Here is a suggestion for revision:

Name_____ Date_____

Paper title_____

Sentence Fluency: how phrases and sentences sound together

See how strong your sentence fluency is and how to make it better.

1	3	5
Beginning (on your mark)	Developing (get set)	Strong (go!)

Here is a suggestion for revision:

Name_____ Date_____

Paper title_____

Conventions: spelling, capitalization, punctuation

See how strong your conventions are and how to make them better.

1	3	5
Beginning (on your mark)	Developing (get set)	Strong (go!)

Here is a suggestion for editing:

Name_____ Date_____

Paper title_____

Presentation: how the writing looks on the page

See how strong your presentation is and how to make it better.

```
        1                    3                    5
●───────●────────────────────●────────────────────●──────────→
   Beginning            Developing             Strong
 (on your mark)        (get set)              (go!)
```

Here is a suggestion for editing:

Name_____ Date_____

Paper title_____

How close is this piece of writing
to being finished and ready to share?

```
        1                    3                    5
●───────●────────────────────●────────────────────●──────────→
   Beginning            Developing             Strong
 (on your mark)        (get set)              (go!)
```

Here is a suggestion for revision and/or editing:

Record-Keeping and Planning Forms

Keeping track of student progress in writing can be a challenge for even the most organized teacher. The forms in this section are designed to help you with this important part of your work by providing simple, ready-to-use blackline masters that will help you document student writing achievement on individual pieces and on a larger collection of work developed over time.

Teacher Contact Record

This handy one-page form can be used to document the writing contacts you have with students, individually and in small groups. One page can capture the interactions you have with each of the students in your class during the course of the year. As the year progresses, you'll want to make sure that you have made time to talk to students about how their writing is developing in all the traits. This form can help you see at a glance where students are having the most trouble, and where you have spent time helping them.

Evidence of the Traits

If you wish to document individual student work over time, try using the Evidence of the Traits page. You will need one for each student and can fill it in as students write new pieces over the year. The form also features a place to document your suggestions and tips to writers so you can keep track of what you have taught them about revision and editing as they go. I recommend dating your comments so you can match them to the paper about which they were made.

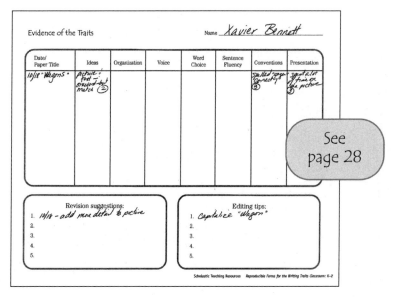

Beginning Writer Continuum and Cover

This continuum pulls all the scoring guides together so you can easily track students' progress on every trait over time. You can assess writing three times a year—beginning, middle, and end—by regularly dating and checking off any indicators that are present in each piece. Over time, you'll notice more and more check marks moving toward the right side of the continuum, sure evidence that the writing is getting stronger. Use the cover sheet to summarize what your continuum scores show and share it with parents or other teachers interested in student writing progress. If you wish, you can put the continuum pages into a folder along with samples of the student's work that you can pass along to next year's teacher.

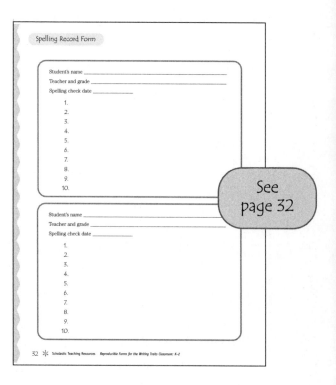

See pages 29–31

Spelling Record Form

Spelling is such a visible part of writing, so to make sure that students and their parents can see how much improvement is taking place in this critical area, select ten grade-appropriate words and ask students to try to spell them at the beginning of the year. In the middle of the year, ask students to spell them again, and finally, as your year together draws to a close, give them one more opportunity to spell the same words. Share the results with students, noticing the improvement. As you talk with parents at conference, set additional goals for spelling words to come the following year.

See page 32

Teacher Contact Record

Dates _____ to _____

Name of student	date/trait	date/trait	date/trait	date/trait	date/trait	date/trait	date/trait	date/trait	date/trait	date/trait	date/trait	date/trait

I = Ideas
O = Organization
V = Voice
WC = Word Choice

SF = Sentence Fluency
C = Conventions
P = Presentation

Scholastic Teaching Resources   Reproducible Forms for the Writing Traits Classroom: K–2

Evidence of the Traits

Name _____

Date/Paper Title	Ideas	Organization	Voice	Word Choice	Sentence Fluency	Conventions	Presentation

Revision suggestions:

1.
2.
3.
4.
5.

Editing tips:

1.
2.
3.
4.
5.

Beginning Writer Continuum and Cover

Student Name _____ Grade _____ Year _____

Teacher _____ School _____

1st Assessment Date _____ Overall Writing Score: 1 2 3 4 5 ⟶ Ready to move to the grades-3-and-up scoring guide

2nd Assessment Date _____ Overall Writing Score: 1 2 3 4 5 ⟶ Ready to move to the grades-3-and-up scoring guide

3rd Assessment Date _____ Overall Writing Score: 1 2 3 4 5 ⟶ Ready to move to the grades-3-and-up scoring guide

(1) Pre-Assessment Goals

(2) Mid-Year Assessment Goals

(3) Final Assessment Goals

Scholastic Teaching Resources Reproducible Forms for the Writing Traits Classroom: K–2

Beginning Writer Continuum

1 Ready to Begin	2 Exploring	3 Expanding	4 Extending	5 Established

IDEAS

1 Ready to Begin	2 Exploring	3 Expanding	4 Extending	5 Established
___ The piece conveys little meaning.	___ One or more ideas are present in the most general way.	___ The idea is written in a basic sentence.	___ The writing works by itself to explain a simple idea or story.	___ The idea is clear and coherent.
___ Real-life objects show up in drawings.	___ Letters and words can be picked out as clues to the topic.	___ A simple statement with somewhat detailed pictures captures the topic.	___ The writing is made up of several sentences on one topic.	___ The text is a well-developed paragraph.
___ Drawings may not be completely recognizable.	___ The drawing helps to clarify the idea.	___ Basic details are present in the text; the illustrations work to enhance the main idea.	___ Key details begin to surface.	___ Elaboration through interesting details creates meaning for the reader.
___ Letters are not consistent or standard.	___ The text is composed of simple, recognizable letters with some early attempts at words.	___ The text contains real words.	___ The writing makes sense, but some information may be missing or irrelevant.	___ The writer shows understanding of the topic through personal experience or research.
___ An oral reading by the writer is needed to understand the message.	___ The reader gets the basic idea but needs the writer's assistance to comprehend it fully.	___ Text and picture are understandable to the reader.	___ Pictures and text work harmoniously to create a rich treatment of the topic.	___ Pictures (if present) enhance the key ideas but aren't necessary for comprehension.

ORGANIZATION

1 Ready to Begin	2 Exploring	3 Expanding	4 Extending	5 Established
___ Letters (if present) are scattered across the page.	___ The piece has no title.	___ The simple title (if present) states the topic.	___ The title (if present) comes close to capturing the central idea.	___ The title (if present) is thoughtful and effective.
___ No coordination of written elements is evident.	___ Letters or words are used as captions.	___ The piece contains a beginning but not a conclusion.	___ The writing starts out strong and includes a predictable ending.	___ There is a clear beginning, middle, and end.
___ Lines, pictures, or letters are randomly placed on the page.	___ Simple clues about order emerge in pictures or text.	___ The piece is little more than a list of sentences connected by a theme.	___ The writer uses a pattern to spotlight the most important details.	___ Important ideas are highlighted within the text.
___ Lines, pictures, or letters are grouped haphazardly.	___ No transitions are indicated.	___ There is basic order with a few missteps.	___ Ideas follow a logical but obvious sequence.	___ Everything fits together nicely.
___ There is no sense of order.	___ The arrangement of pictures or text shows an awareness of the importance of structure and pattern.	___ There is more text at the beginning than in the middle or end.	___ The writing's pace is even; it doesn't bog the reader down.	___ The text slows down and speeds up to highlight the ideas and shows the writer's skill at pacing.
	___ Left-to-right, top-to-bottom orientation is evident.	___ Sentence parts are linked with conjunctions (but, and, or).	___ Basic transitions link one sentence to the next.	___ Clear transitions connect one sentence to the next.

VOICE

1 Ready to Begin	2 Exploring	3 Expanding	4 Extending	5 Established
___ The reader is not sure why the writer chose this idea for writing.	___ The piece is routine response to the assignment.	___ There are fleeting glimpses of how the writer looks at the topic.	___ The writer takes a standard topic and addresses it in a nonstandard way.	___ The writer "owns" the topic.
___ The writer tries to copy without purpose what he or she sees around the room.	___ The writer copies environmental text but also adds an original bit.	___ Touches of originality are found in text and pictures.	___ The writer tries a new word, interesting image, or unusual detail.	___ The piece contains the writer's imprint.
___ No awareness of audience is evident.	___ The text connects with the reader in the most general way.	___ There is a moment of audience awareness, but then it fades.	___ The writing speaks to the reader in several places.	___ The writer is mindful of the piece's audience and connects purposefully with the reader.
___ The piece contains very simple drawings or lines.	___ The drawings begin to reveal the individual.	___ BIG letters, exclamation points, underlining, repetition, and pictures are used for emphasis.	___ The writing captures a general mood such as happy, sad, or mad.	___ The tone is identifiable—bittersweet, compassionate, frustrated, terrified, and so on.
___ Nothing distinguishes the work to make it the writer's own.	___ The barest hint of the writer is in evidence.	___ A pat summary statement conceals the writer's individuality.	___ The writer begins to show how he or she really thinks and feels about the topic.	___ The writer takes real risks, creating a truly individual piece of writing.

Beginning Writer Continuum

1 Ready to Begin	2 Exploring	3 Expanding	4 Extending	5 Established
WORD CHOICE	**WORD CHOICE**	**WORD CHOICE**	**WORD CHOICE**	**WORD CHOICE**
— Scribbling and random lines mark the page. — Imitation letters may be present. — There may be random strings of letters across the page. — Writer uses his or her name. — Few, if any, recognizable words are present.	— Conventional letters are present. — The letter strings begin to form words. — Letter strings can be read as words even though the spacing and spelling isn't correct. — Words from the board, displays, or word walls are attempted. — A few words can be identified.	— Some words make sense. — The reader begins to see what the writer is describing. — One or two words stand out. — Occasional misuse of words bogs the reader down. — The writer tries out new words.	— Descriptive nouns (e.g., Raisin Bran, not cereal) are combined with generic ones. — The writer uses an active verb or two. — There is very little repetition of words. — The writer attempts figurative language. — The writer "stretches" by using different types of words.	— The writer uses everyday words and phrases with a fresh and original spin. — The words paint a clear picture in the reader's mind. — The writer uses just the right words or phrase. — Figurative language works reasonably well. — Colorful words are used correctly and with creativity.
SENTENCE FLUENCY	**SENTENCE FLUENCY**	**SENTENCE FLUENCY**	**SENTENCE FLUENCY**	**SENTENCE FLUENCY**
— It's hard to figure out how the elements go together. — Words, if present, stand alone. — Imitation words and letters are used across the page. — There is no overall sense of flow to the piece. — Only the writer can read the piece aloud.	— Written elements work together in units. — Words are combined to make short, repetitive phrases. — Awkward word patterns break the flow of the piece. — The reader gets only one or two clues about how the pictures and text are connected. — The writer stumbles when reading the text aloud and may have to back up and reread.	— Basic subject-verb agreement occurs in simple sentences—e.g., "I jumped." — Sentence beginnings are identical, making all sentences sound alike. — Longer sentences go on and on. — Simple conjunctions such as *and* and *but* are used to make compound sentences. — The piece is easy to read aloud, although it may contain repetitive or awkward sentence patterns.	— Sentences are of different lengths. — Sentences start differently. — Some sentences read smoothly while others still need work. — Connectives are correctly used in long and short sentences. — Aside from a couple of awkward moments, the piece can be read aloud easily.	— Different sentence lengths give the writing a nice sound. There is playfulness and experimentation. — Varied sentence beginnings create a pleasing rhythm. — The piece is a breeze to read aloud. — Different kinds of sentences (statements, commands, questions, and exclamations) are present. — The flow from one sentence to the next is smooth.
CONVENTIONS	**CONVENTIONS**	**CONVENTIONS**	**CONVENTIONS**	**CONVENTIONS**
— Letters are written in strings (pre-phonetic spelling—e.g., *gGmkrRt*). — Letters are formed irregularly; there is no intentional use of upper- and lowercase letters. — Spacing is uneven between letters and words. — Punctuation is not present. — The piece does not employ standard conventions.	— The words are unreadable to the untrained eye (quasi-phonetic spelling—e.g., *KN, sD, Wt*). — There is little discrimination between upper- and lowercase letters. — Spacing between letters and words is present. — The writer experiments with punctuation. — The use of conventions is not consistent.	— Spelling is inconsistent (phonetic spelling—e.g., *kitn, sed, wtn*) but readable. — Upper- and lowercase letters are used correctly. — Capitals mark the beginning of sentences. — End punctuation marks are generally used correctly. — The writing correctly follows simple conventions.	— Spelling is correct or close on high-use words (*kiten, soed, want*). — Sentence beginnings and proper nouns are capitalized. — The writer uses end punctuation and series commas correctly. — The writer may try more advanced punctuation (dashes, ellipses, quotation marks) but not always with success. — Only minor editing is required to show thoughtful use of conventions.	— High-use words are spelled correctly and others are easy to read. — The writer applies basic capitalization rules with consistency. — Punctuation marks are used effectively to guide the reader. — One or more paragraphs with indenting are present. — Standard English grammar is used. — Conventions are applied consistently and accurately.

Spelling Record Form

Student's name _____

Teacher and grade _____

Spelling check date _____

    1.

    2.

    3.

    4.

    5.

    6.

    7.

    8.

    9.

  10.

Student's name _____

Teacher and grade _____

Spelling check date _____

    1.

    2.

    3.

    4.

    5.

    6.

    7.

    8.

    9.

  10.

Parent Communication

Teaching parents about the traits helps them provide constructive writing support at home. In this section, you'll find some ideas for showing parents just what to do to help their child become a strong and independent writer.

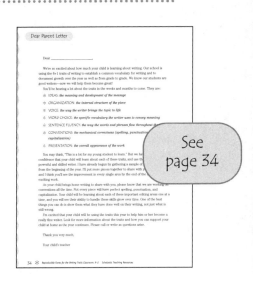

See page 34

Dear Parent Letter

Parents appreciate ideas on how to help their child with writing. However, parents often comment that they don't know how to begin, so this letter may help you set the stage for a collaborative process that begins at school and is followed up at home. You'll be sharing more information with parents about the traits during the year, but in this letter, you give them a place to begin thinking about the traits and how you plan to use them to help teach their child to write.

Trait Support at Home

Parents can use this form to talk to their child about their writing, focusing on one trait at a time. The forms can be addressed to a parent, brother or sister, or other person who helps the child outside of school. Attach a form to the writing, and send it home so the family member can interact positively and quickly with the child about their writing, filling in answers to the questions as they go. Ask students to bring the completed form and their writing back to school so they can consider revising and editing their work to include suggestions made by their parents or other writing coach.

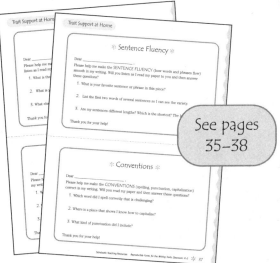

See pages 35–38

Activities to Encourage Writing at Home

Imagine all the different ways to helps students engage in literacy activities—there must be hundreds of them. Use this resource list to spur parents into action by including reading and writing as a critical part of life with their children at home.

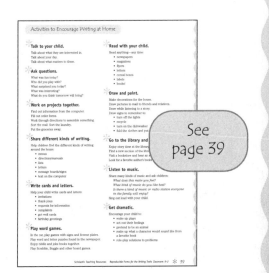

See page 39

Dear _____,

We're so excited about how much your child is learning about writing. Our school is using the 6+1 traits of writing to establish a common vocabulary for writing and to document growth over the year as well as from grade to grade. We know our students are good writers—now we will help them become great!

You'll be hearing a lot about the traits in the weeks and months to come. They are:

* IDEAS: *the meaning and development of the message*

* ORGANIZATION: *the internal structure of the piece*

* VOICE: *the way the writer brings the topic to life*

* WORD CHOICE: *the specific vocabulary the writer uses to convey meaning*

* SENTENCE FLUENCY: *the way the words and phrases flow throughout the text*

* CONVENTIONS: *the mechanical correctness (spelling, punctuation, capitalization)*

* PRESENTATION: *the overall appearance of the work*

You may think, "This is a lot for my young student to learn." But we have every confidence that your child will learn about each of these traits, and use them to become a powerful and skilled writer. I have already begun by gathering a sample of your child's work from the beginning of the year. I'll put more pieces together to share with you over the year, and I think you'll see the improvement in every single area by the end of the school year. It's exciting work.

As your child brings home writing to share with you, please know that we are working on conventions all the time. Not every piece will have perfect spelling, punctuation, and capitalization. Your child will be learning about each of these important editing areas one at a time, and you will see their ability to handle these skills grow over time. One of the best things you can do is show them what they have done well on their writing, not just what is still wrong.

I'm excited that your child will be using the traits this year to help him or her become a really fine writer. Look for more information about the traits and how you can support your child at home as the year continues. Please call or write as questions arise.

Thank you very much,

Your child's teacher

✳ Ideas ✳

Dear _____ ,

Please help me make the IDEA (the main message) clear in my writing. Will you listen as I read my paper to you and then answer these questions?

1. What is the main idea of this piece?

2. What is your favorite detail?

3. What else should I add to make my idea clear?

Thank you for your help!

✳ Organization ✳

Dear _____ ,

Please help me make the ORGANIZATION (the order and structure) work well in my writing. Will you listen as I read my paper to you and then answer these questions?

1. What do you like about my beginning?

2. Which words show that I have put my details in a logical order?

3. How well does the ending wrap up this piece?

Thank you for your help!

❋ Voice ❋

Dear _____ ,

Please help me make the VOICE (my personal style) stand out in my writing. Will you listen as I read my paper to you and then answer these questions?

1. What words and phrases did I use that sound like me?

2. Is there one place in my writing that you think has the most voice?

3. What did I do that shows how much I care about this topic?

Thank you for your help!

❋ Word Choice ❋

Dear _____ ,

Please help me make the WORD CHOICE (colorful and interesting words) work well in my writing. Will you listen as I read my paper to you and then answer these questions?

1. What is your favorite word or phrase in this piece?

2. What verb stands out?

3 Where did I write so clearly you got a picture in your mind?

Thank you for your help!

✳ Sentence Fluency ✳

Dear _____ ,

Please help me make the SENTENCE FLUENCY (how words and phrases flow) smooth in my writing. Will you listen as I read my paper to you and then answer these questions?

1. What is your favorite sentence or phrase in this piece?

2. List the first two words of several sentences so I can see the variety.

3. Are my sentences different lengths? Which is the shortest? The longest?

Thank you for your help!

✳ Conventions ✳

Dear _____ ,

Please help me make the CONVENTIONS (spelling, punctuation, capitalization) correct in my writing. Will you read my paper and then answer these questions?

1. Which word did I spell correctly that is challenging?

2. Where is a place that shows I know how to capitalize?

3. What kind of punctuation did I include?

Thank you for your help!

✳ Presentation ✳

Dear _____ ,

Please help me make the PRESENTATION (the overall appearance) stand out in my writing. Will you look at my paper and then answer these questions?

1. Where have I used white space well?

2. Which line shows my best handwriting?

3. Is this copy easy to read or are there still cross-out and smudges you can point out so I can clean them up?

Thank you for your help!

✳ All Traits ✳

Dear _____ ,

Please help me make my writing as strong as possible. Will you listen as I read my paper to you and then answer these questions?

1. What is something I did well on this piece?

2. What is something you think I should work on?

3. Did I do something new that shows how much I am learning about writing? What was it?

Thank you for your help!

Activities to Encourage Writing at Home

Talk to your child.

Talk about what they are interested in.
Talk about your day.
Talk about what matters to them.

Ask questions.

What was fun today?
Who did you play with?
What surprised you today?
What was interesting?
What do you think tomorrow will bring?

Work on projects together.

Find out information from the computer.
Fill out order forms.
Work through directions to assemble something.
Sort the mail. Sort the laundry.
Put the groceries away.

Share different kinds of writing.

Help children find the different kinds of writing around the house:

- menus
- directions/manuals
- lists
- letters
- message boards/signs
- text on the computer

Write cards and letters.

Help your child write cards and letters:

- invitations
- thank-yous
- requests for information
- complaints
- get-well cards
- birthday greetings

Play word games.

In the car, play games with signs and license plates.
Play word and letter puzzles found in the newspaper.
Enjoy riddle and joke books together.
Play Scrabble, Boggle, and other board games.

Read with your child.

Read anything—any time:

- newspapers
- magazines
- flyers
- letters
- cereal boxes
- labels
- books!

Draw and paint.

Make decorations for the house.
Draw pictures to mail to friends and relatives.
Draw while listening to a story.
Draw signs to remember to:

- turn off the lights
- recycle
- turn on the dishwasher
- fold the clothes and put them away

Go to the library and bookstore.

Enjoy story time at the library and check out books.
Find a new section of the library and browse.
Visit a bookstore and hear an author read a book.
Look for a favorite author's books on the bookstore shelves.

Listen to music.

Share many kinds of music and ask children:
What does this make you feel?
What kind of music do you like best?
Is there a kind of music or radio station everyone in the family will enjoy?
Sing out loud with your child.

Get dramatic.

Encourage your child to:

- make up plays
- act out their feelings
- pretend to be an animal
- make up what a character would sound like from a favorite book
- role-play solutions to problems

Reproducible Writing Traits Forms for Students

The second half of this book contains forms that students can use 1) to monitor their own progress in writing and 2) for support to learn and apply the writing process. Like all writers, primary students thrive when they see for themselves what they are doing well and can measure their own progress. It's motivating and encouraging—two keys to success.

Primary students who learn the traits develop powerful insights into what makes writing work. They develop skills in revision and editing, two cornerstones of the writing process, and they get an insider's perspective on what to do to improve writing over time. These are useful tools in the writer's toolbox, and they are based, in part, in the young writer's understanding of the traits.

The forms that follow in this section are designed to make your work with students easier and more purposeful. As students gain appreciation for how the traits and the writing process work together, they take big steps toward becoming self-motivated—a lifelong skill every teacher is delighted to see develop in his or her young writers.

Student-Friendly Scoring Guides and Scoring Help

Student-Friendly Scoring Guides

Give students their own copy of the student-friendly scoring guides.* As they write, point out the trait or traits you want them to focus on and ask them to assess their own writing before they share it with you. Students who don't see their writing as strong will need specific ideas on how to improve it, but the assessment is the first step along that path. Recognizing strengths and weaknesses in writing is an important skill all writers must master. You should wait to give students their own scoring guide until you are confident they can read and understand this amount of text, however. These student-friendly guides may most appropriately be used at the end of first grade and into second.

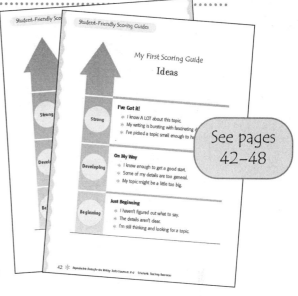

See pages 42–48

Student Writing Cumulative Scoring Sheet

Ask students to write the title of each piece of their writing along the left side of this form in the space provided. Then, encourage them to keep track of their scores by circling each that is assigned to that piece. If just a few traits were assessed on a paper, tell them it is fine to circle only those that were given scores. After a few papers, students will begin to see patterns in their score, and hopefully, over time, they will see the numbers improve.

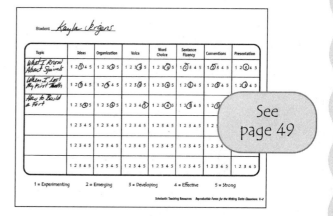

See page 49

Self-Evaluation and Reflection Form

Cut these forms apart and use them to spur students' thinking about what they have done well and what still needs work on their papers. As students learn to think about their writing, they will see a place for application of each of the traits. It's important to allow students time to reflect on what they have learned. You'll gain valuable insights into what they know by looking at these reflection forms, too.

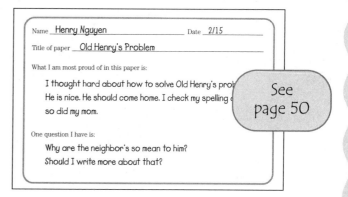

See page 50

---

* As found in *6+1 Traits of Writing: The Complete Guide for the Primary Grades*, Scholastic, 2005

My First Scoring Guide

Ideas

Strong

I've Got it!

* ✳ I know A LOT about this topic.
* ✳ My writing is bursting with fascinating details.
* ✳ I've picked a topic small enough to handle.

Developing

On My Way

* ✳ I know enough to get a good start.
* ✳ Some of my details are too general.
* ✳ My topic might be a little too big.

Beginning

Just Beginning

* ✳ I haven't figured out what to say.
* ✳ The details aren't clear.
* ✳ I'm still thinking and looking for a topic.

My First Scoring Guide
Organization

Strong

I've Got It!

* I have a bold beginning, mighty middle, and excellent ending.
* My details are in the right places.
* I've given my ideas an order that really works.

Developing

On My Way

* I've made a good start at a beginning, middle, and ending.
* Most of my details fit.
* The order of my ideas makes sense.

Beginning

Just Beginning

* My writing doesn't have a clear beginning, middle, or ending.
* My details are jumbled and confusing.
* I have "stuff" on paper, but it's not in order.

My First Scoring Guide

Voice

I've Got It!

Strong

* My writing sounds like me.
* The reader will know I care about this topic.
* I have the right amount of energy in this piece.

On My Way

Developing

* My writing is safe. You only get a glimpse of me.
* I have only a passing interest in this topic.
* My energy level is uneven in this piece.

Just Beginning

Beginning

* I forgot to add what I think and feel in this piece.
* I really don't care at all about this topic.
* I'm bored and it shows.

My First Scoring Guide
Word Choice

Strong

I've Got It!

* I've picked exactly the right words.
* My words are colorful, fresh, and snappy.
* The words help my reader see my ideas.

Developing

On My Way

* Some of my words work well, but others don't.
* I've used too many ordinary words.
* My words paint a general picture of the idea.

Beginning

Just Beginning

* I'm confused about how to use words well.
* I've left out key words.
* Many of my words are the same or just wrong.

My First Scoring Guide

Sentence Fluency

Strong

I've Got It!

* My sentences are well-built and easy to read aloud.
* The way my sentences begin makes them interesting.
* I've varied my sentence lengths.

Developing

On My Way

* I've got sentences! Some of them are hard to read aloud, though.
* I've tried a couple of different ways to begin my sentences.
* I might put some sentences together or I could cut a few in two.

Beginning

Just Beginning

* I am having trouble making a sentence.
* My beginnings all sound the same.
* I've used *and* too many times or many sentences are too short.

My First Scoring Guide

Conventions

Strong

I've Got It!

* ✳ My spelling is magnificent.
* ✳ All my capitals are in the right places.
* ✳ I used punctuation correctly to make my writing easy to read.
* ✳ I've used correct grammar and added paragraphs where needed.
* ✳ I've done a great job proofreading.

Developing

On My Way

* ✳ Only my simpler words are spelled correctly.
* ✳ I've used capitals in easy spots.
* ✳ I have correct punctuation in some places, but not in others.
* ✳ I proofread quickly and missed some things.

Beginning

Just Beginning

* ✳ It's hard to read my words because of the spelling.
* ✳ My capitals don't follow the rules.
* ✳ I haven't used punctuation well at all.
* ✳ I forgot to proofread.

My First Scoring Guide

Presentation

Strong

I've Got it!

* My paper is neat—no smudges or cross-outs.
* My letters are printed and written clearly.
* I have margins that make a frame.

Developing

On My Way

* My paper can be read, but it's not my best.
* Some of my letters are well done, but some are not.
* My margins work better in some places but not in others.

Beginning

Just Beginning

* My paper is very hard to read.
* My letters are a mess.
* I forgot to use margins.

Student Writing Cumulative Scoring Sheet

Student _____

Topic	Ideas	Organization	Voice	Word Choice	Sentence Fluency	Conventions	Presentation
	1 2 3 4 5	1 2 3 4 5	1 2 3 4 5	1 2 3 4 5	1 2 3 4 5	1 2 3 4 5	1 2 3 4 5
	1 2 3 4 5	1 2 3 4 5	1 2 3 4 5	1 2 3 4 5	1 2 3 4 5	1 2 3 4 5	1 2 3 4 5
	1 2 3 4 5	1 2 3 4 5	1 2 3 4 5	1 2 3 4 5	1 2 3 4 5	1 2 3 4 5	1 2 3 4 5
	1 2 3 4 5	1 2 3 4 5	1 2 3 4 5	1 2 3 4 5	1 2 3 4 5	1 2 3 4 5	1 2 3 4 5
	1 2 3 4 5	1 2 3 4 5	1 2 3 4 5	1 2 3 4 5	1 2 3 4 5	1 2 3 4 5	1 2 3 4 5
	1 2 3 4 5	1 2 3 4 5	1 2 3 4 5	1 2 3 4 5	1 2 3 4 5	1 2 3 4 5	1 2 3 4 5

1 = Experimenting   2 = Emerging   3 = Developing   4 = Effective   5 = Strong

Scholastic Teaching Resources   Reproducible Forms for the Writing Traits Classroom: K–2

Self-Evaluation and Reflection Form

Name _____ Date _____

Title of paper _____

What I am most proud of in this paper is:

One question I have is:

Name _____ Date _____

Title of paper _____

What I am most proud of in this paper is:

One question I have is:

The Writing Process:
Drafting, Revising, and Editing

Bring the writing process to life in your primary classroom by showing students how to use the traits to guide them as they write. The first five traits—ideas, organization, voice, word choice, and sentence fluency—are the revision traits. These areas are what writers think about and clarify in their writing as they work to make it as strong as possible. The last two traits, conventions and presentation, are what writers look at when they edit. This is where the writing is prepared for the reader using standard conventions and formatting. Students who learn the difference between revision and editing have insider's knowledge on the writing process, the cornerstone to successful writing at any age.

Sharing My Writing Paper Clippers

Use these observations about writing to reinforce what is going well in student work. Copy these forms, cut them apart, and encourage students to use the ones that reflect the traits they are working on when they get ready to turn in papers or have a teacher or peer conference. Each trait is represented, so you can use one or more, depending on how many traits your students can handle at a time. Notice that each comment requires some action on the part of students to check their own work for the trait. Over time, students will internalize these revision and editing actions and be able to apply them with ease.

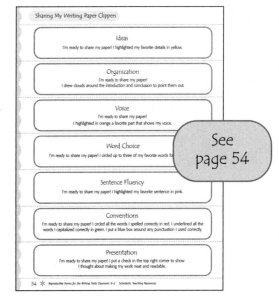

See page 54

Quick Checks for the Traits

Learning to use the traits to improve writing becomes a doable task for young writers when they use these Quick Checks. Each one is keyed to a particular trait, and the writer is asked to check off any of the qualities of that trait that they have included in their writing. Not only is this a good way to make sure the writing is as strong as possible before it is turned in, it builds understanding of what the traits are as students use this handy set of forms.

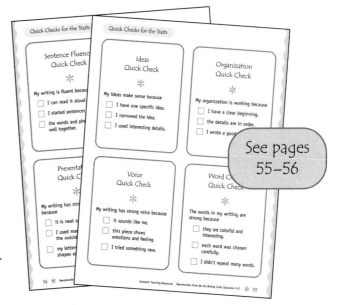

See pages 55–56

Trait Songs

Students and teachers alike appreciate having a copy of the delightful trait songs to sing as they work together in the writing classroom. Each of the songs has new words set to a familiar tune, so singing them will be a breeze. Once students have mastered these songs, encourage them to write new stanzas that show even more information about each of the traits.

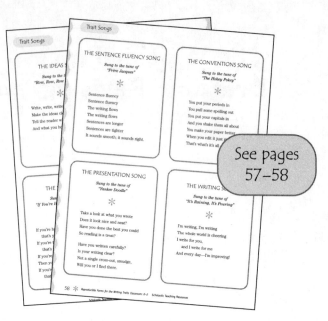

See pages 57–58

Writing Process Steps

Learning how to use the writing process is an important step in a primary writer's development. Although revision may be physically and mentally challenging for the youngest writers, you can begin by showing students the possibilities with this form. With practice, your primary students will be able to complete all the steps on this form. But it's a good idea to start with one question and focus on the skills related to just one trait. Move on from there as students become more comfortable revising their work over time.

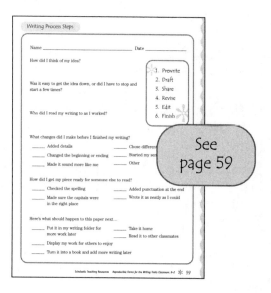

See page 59

Editor Alert

Your young writers will appreciate having a copy of these editing symbols to use in their own work. They can apply one at a time as you teach them, and learn to edit their work so it is polished and easy to read. Use the Editor Alert checklist when students have learned these important skills and can check their own or a peer's work, making it as conventionally correct as possible.

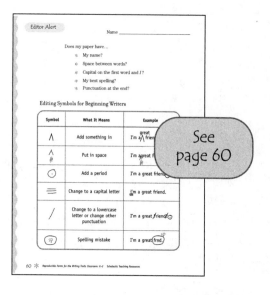

See page 60

Peer Conference Guide

Students can help each other with revision and editing by consulting these simple conference guide questions on each trait as they go. Run off all the peer revision guide forms and ask students to select the one that matches the trait they will talk about with their partner during writing workshop. These forms will provide structure for the peer conference.

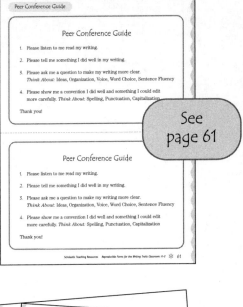

See page 61

Graphic Organizers for Each Trait

Graphic organizers are a great way to help students visualize and remember information. Here I present seven different graphic organizers, one per trait, that you can make into transparencies and use as springboards into writing lessons:

* Fun With Funnels helps students narrow their idea.
* Break It Down encourages students to organize their writing thoughtfully.
* Matching Voices helps students choose a voice for their piece.
* Different Way to Say. . . helps students expand their word choice.
* Mix It Up encourages students to experiment with different sentence structures.
* "I Can" Editing List provides a place for young writers to note different conventions skills they have mastered.
* Frame It reminds students what they need to do to prepare a paper for an audience.

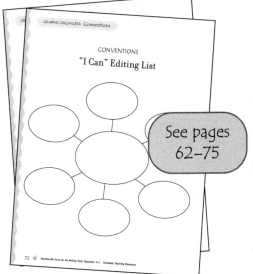

See pages 62–75

Students can use the graphic organizers on their own as they're writing. I provide a blank graphic organizer and a filled-in model for each of the traits. I recommend making an overhead of the filled-in example so students can see the possibilities for completing their own. Share the blank version in small groups and discuss how the graphic organizer helps them to focus on one quality of the trait. Ask students to apply what the graphic organizer showed to a piece of their own writing as they revise it and make it stronger.

Stationery

Match the level of writing development of your students—from simple letters and sounds to multiple sentence—to the four types of paper provided. The first allows students to draw and simply write letters or sounds that they think go with the picture. The second provides a place for students to write a whole word or title for the picture. The third gives a place for a sentence to accompany the picture. The fourth, pictured here, allows for the most writing to go with the picture.

See pages 76–79

Ideas

I'm ready to share my paper! I highlighted my favorite details in yellow.

Organization

I'm ready to share my paper!
I drew clouds around the introduction and conclusion to point them out.

Voice

I'm ready to share my paper!
I highlighted in orange a favorite part that shows my voice.

Word Choice

I'm ready to share my paper! I circled up to three of my favorite words for you to enjoy.

Sentence Fluency

I'm ready to share my paper! I highlighted my favorite sentence in pink.

Conventions

I'm ready to share my paper! I circled all the words I spelled correctly in red. I underlined all the words I capitalized correctly in green. I put a blue box around any punctuation I used correctly.

Presentation

I'm ready to share my paper! I put a check in the top right corner to show
I thought about making my work neat and readable.

Ideas
Quick Check

✳

My ideas make sense because

☐ I have one specific idea.

☐ I narrowed the idea.

☐ I used interesting details.

Organization
Quick Check

✳

My organization is working because

☐ I have a clear beginning.

☐ the details are in order.

☐ I wrote a good ending.

Voice
Quick Check

✳

My writing has strong voice because

☐ it sounds like me.

☐ this piece shows emotions and feeling.

☐ I tried something new.

Word Choice
Quick Check

✳

The words in my writing are strong because

☐ they are colorful and interesting.

☐ each word was chosen carefully.

☐ I didn't repeat many words.

Sentence Fluency Quick Check

✳

My writing is fluent because

- ☐ I can read it aloud easily.
- ☐ I started sentences differently.
- ☐ the words and phrases work well together.

Conventions Quick Check

✳

My writing is edited because

- ☐ I checked the spelling.
- ☐ I added punctuation at the end.
- ☐ I made sure to use capital letters with *I* and at the beginning of sentences.

Presentation Quick Check

✳

My writing has strong presentation because

- ☐ it is neat and readable.
- ☐ I used margins around the outside.
- ☐ my letters are all the right shapes and sizes.

My Writing Quick Check

✳

You will enjoy reading this piece because

- ☐ I wrote about something I care about.
- ☐ you'll find out something new.
- ☐ I used conventions to make it easy to read.

THE IDEAS SONG

*Sung to the tune of
"Row, Row, Row Your Boat"*

Write, write, write your thoughts
Make the ideas clear
Tell the reader what you know
And what you hold most dear.

THE ORGANIZATION SONG

*Sung to the tune of
"Mary Had a Little Lamb"*

Writing has a good beginning,
strong conclusion,
and builds bridges
Writing has a good beginning
The order just makes sense.

THE VOICE SONG

*Sung to the tune of
"If You're Happy and You Know It"*

If you're happy and you know it—
that's your voice
If you're thoughtful and you know it—
that's your voice
If you're spunky and you know it,
Then your words will surely show it
If you're happy and you know it—
that's your voice.

THE WORD CHOICE SONG

*Sung to the tune of
"Ring Around the Rosie"*

Writing with your best words
Finding lots of new words
Sparkle! Dazzle!
The words stand out.

THE SENTENCE FLUENCY SONG

Sung to the tune of
"Frère Jacques"

Sentence fluency
Sentence fluency
The writing flows
The writing flows
Sentences are longer
Sentences are tighter
It sounds smooth; it sounds right.

THE CONVENTIONS SONG

Sung to the tune of
"The Hokey Pokey"

You put your periods in
You pull some spelling out
You put your capitals in
And you shake them all about
You make your paper better
When you edit it just right
That's what's it's all about.

THE PRESENTATION SONG

Sung to the tune of
"Yankee Doodle"

Take a look at what you wrote
Does it look nice and neat?
Have you done the best you could
So reading is a treat?

Have you written carefully?
Is your writing clear?
Not a single cross-out, smudge,
Will you or I find there.

THE WRITING SONG

Sung to the tune of
"It's Raining, It's Pouring"

I'm writing, I'm writing
The whole world is cheering
I write for you,
    and I write for me
And every day—I'm improving!

Name _____ Date _____

How did I think of my idea?

Was it easy to get the idea down, or did I have to stop and start a few times?

Who did I read my writing to as I worked?

1. Prewrite
2. Draft
3. Share
4. Revise
5. Edit
6. Finish

What changes did I make before I finished my writing?

_____ Added details   _____ Chose different words

_____ Changed the beginning or ending   _____ Started my sentences differently

_____ Made it sound more like me   _____ Other

How did I get my piece ready for someone else to read?

_____ Checked the spelling   _____ Added punctuation at the end

_____ Made sure the capitals were   _____ Wrote it as neatly as I could
       in the right place

Here's what should happen to this paper next…

_____ Put it in my writing folder for   _____ Take it home
       more work later
                                             _____ Read it to other classmates

_____ Display my work for others to enjoy

_____ Turn it into a book and add more writing later

Name _____

Does my paper have…

     ✳   My name?

     ✳   Space between words?

     ✳   Capital on the first word and *I* ?

     ✳   My best spelling?

     ✳   Punctuation at the end?

Editing Symbols for Beginning Writers

Symbol	What It Means	Example
∧	Add something in	great I'm a ∧ friend.
∧ #	Put in space	I'm agreat friend. #
⊙	Add a period	I'm a great friend ⊙
≡	Change to a capital letter	i'm a great friend.
/	Change to a lowercase letter or change other punctuation	I'm a great friend? ⊙
sp	Spelling mistake	sp I'm a great (frnd.)

Peer Conference Guide: Revision

1. Please listen to me read my writing.

2. Please tell me something I did well in my writing.

3. Please circle one of these revision traits:

   Ideas   Organization   Voice   Word Choice   Sentence Fluency

   Ask me a question about this trait to help me make my writing stronger.

Thank you!

Peer Conference Guide: Editing

1. Please look at my writing with me as I read it aloud.

2. Please tell me something I did well in my writing.

3. Please circle one of these editing issues for the conventions traits:

   Spelling   Punctuation   Capitalization

   Show me one thing I did well with this trait and one place I could make it stronger.

Thank you!

IDEAS

Fun With Funnels

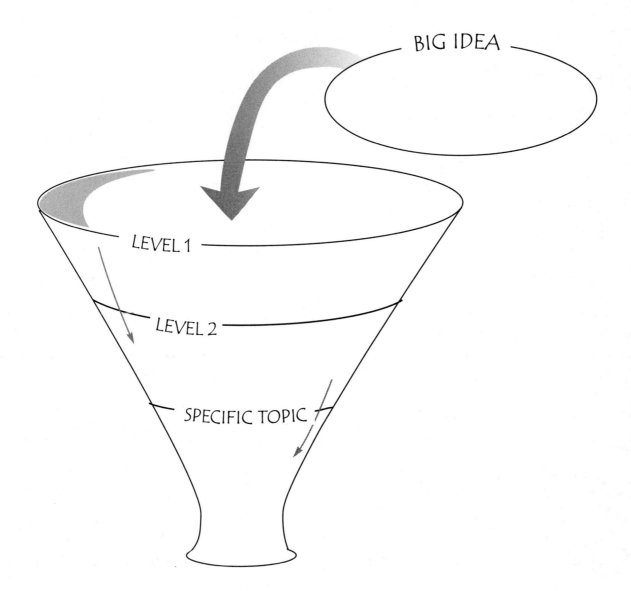

BIG IDEA

LEVEL 1

LEVEL 2

SPECIFIC TOPIC

Details about my specific topic:

IDEAS

Fun With Funnels

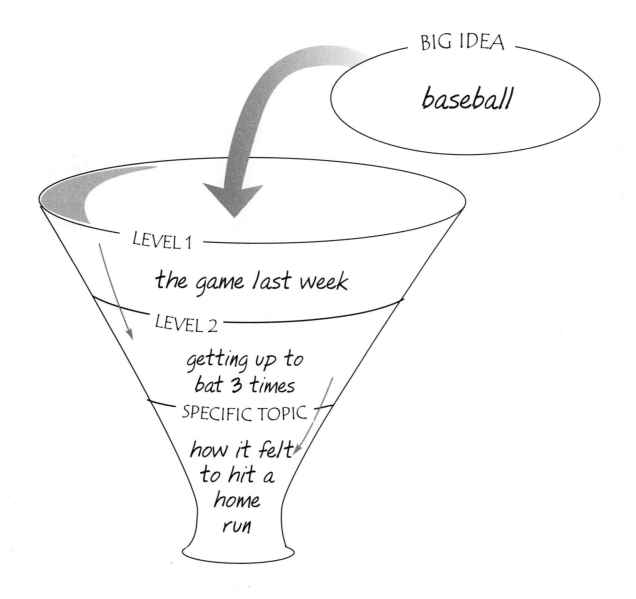

BIG IDEA

baseball

LEVEL 1

the game last week

LEVEL 2

getting up to bat 3 times

SPECIFIC TOPIC

how it felt to hit a home run

Details about my specific topic:

ORGANIZATION

Break It Down

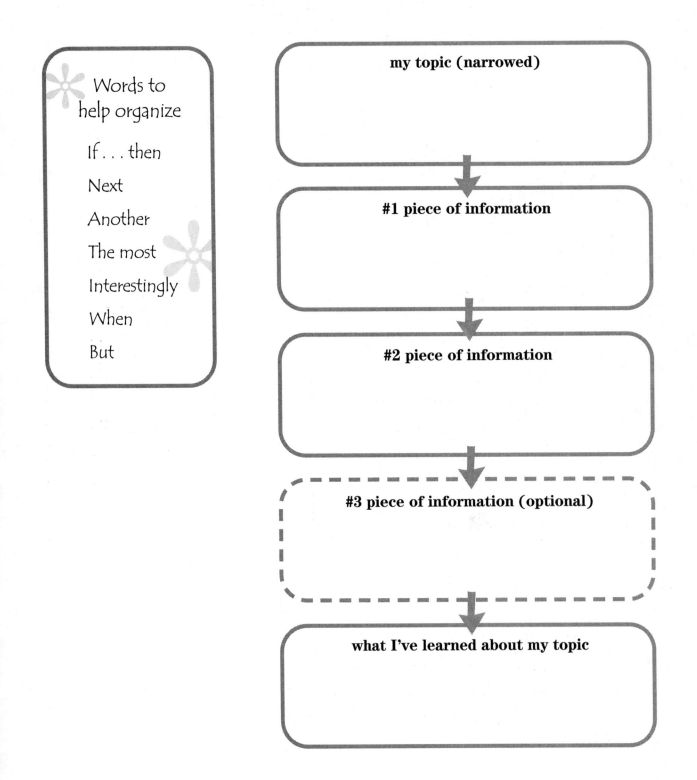

Words to help organize

If . . . then

Next

Another

The most

Interestingly

When

But

my topic (narrowed)

#1 piece of information

#2 piece of information

#3 piece of information (optional)

what I've learned about my topic

ORGANIZATION

Break It Down

Words to help organize

If . . . then

Next

Another

The most

Interestingly

When

But

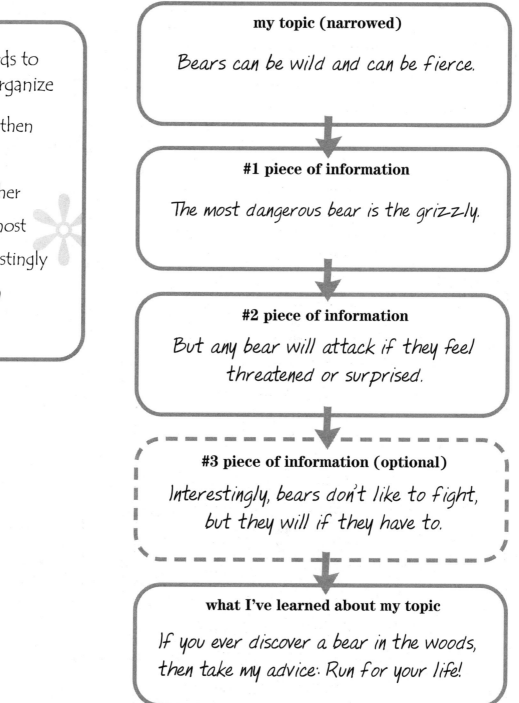

my topic (narrowed)

Bears can be wild and can be fierce.

#1 piece of information

The most dangerous bear is the grizzly.

#2 piece of information

But any bear will attack if they feel threatened or surprised.

#3 piece of information (optional)

Interestingly, bears don't like to fight, but they will if they have to.

what I've learned about my topic

If you ever discover a bear in the woods, then take my advice: Run for your life!

VOICE

Matching Voices

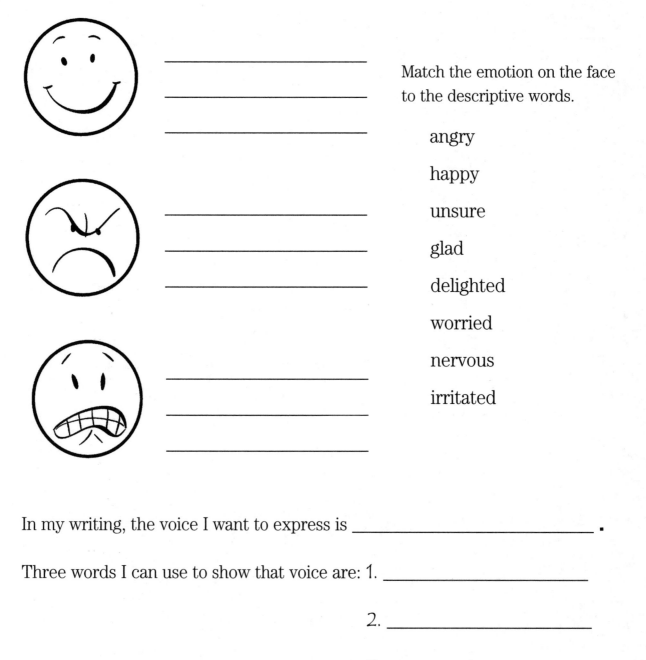

Match the emotion on the face
to the descriptive words.

angry

happy

unsure

glad

delighted

worried

nervous

irritated

In my writing, the voice I want to express is _____ .

Three words I can use to show that voice are: 1. _____

2. _____

3. _____

VOICE

Matching Voices

_____ happy _____
_____ glad _____
_____ delighted _____

Match the emotion on the face to the descriptive words.

angry

happy

_____ angry _____
_____ irritated _____
_____

unsure

glad

delighted

worried

nervous

_____ unsure _____
_____ worried _____
_____ nervous _____

irritated

In my writing, the voice I want to express is _____ enthusiastic _____ .

Three words I can use to show that voice are: 1. _____ excited _____

2. _____ eager _____

3. _____ thrilled _____

WORD CHOICE

Different Way to Say . . .

Other words to try

WORD CHOICE

Different Way to Say . . .

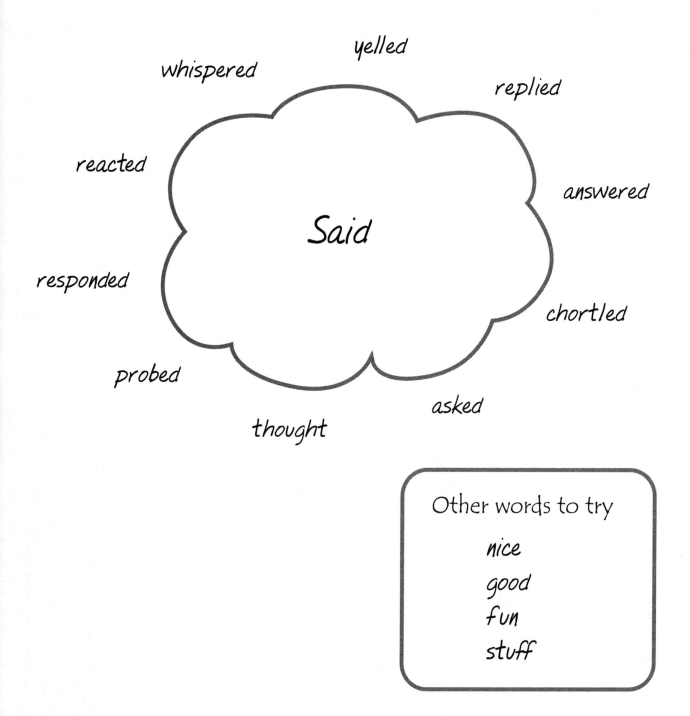

yelled

whispered

replied

reacted

answered

Said

responded

chortled

probed

asked

thought

Other words to try

nice

good

fun

stuff

SENTENCE FLUENCY

Mix It Up

Basic sentence:

1. Switch Around:

2. Simplify:

3. Stretch It Out:

Try it:
1. Switch words around.
2. Simplify.
3. Stretch it out.

SENTENCE FLUENCY

Mix It Up

Basic sentence:

Dinosaurs are the most fascinating, interesting animals.

1. Switch Around:

Of all the animals, dinosaurs are the most fascinating and interesting.

2. Simplify:

Dinosaurs are fascinating and interesting.

3. Stretch It Out:

Some people like dogs, cats, or birds, but I think dinosaurs are the most fascinating and interesting animals to study.

Try it:
1. Switch words around.
2. Simplify.
3. Stretch it out.

CONVENTIONS

"I Can" Editing List

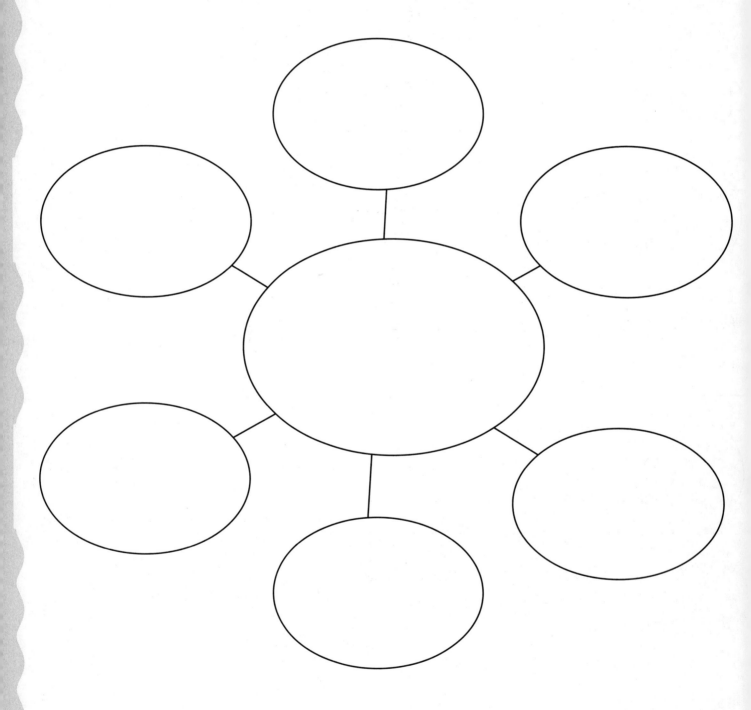

CONVENTIONS
"I Can" Editing List

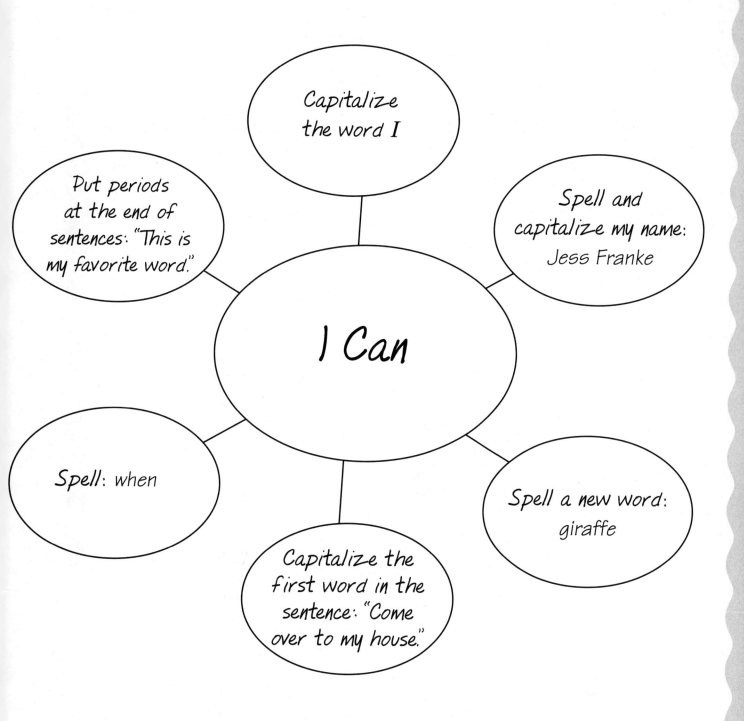

PRESENTATION

Frame It

My writing is easy to read when:

1.

2.

3.

4.

PRESENTATION

Frame It

My writing is easy to read when:

1. I use margins.

2. I write neatly.

3. I use spacing.

4. I take my time.

Stationery

Name: _____

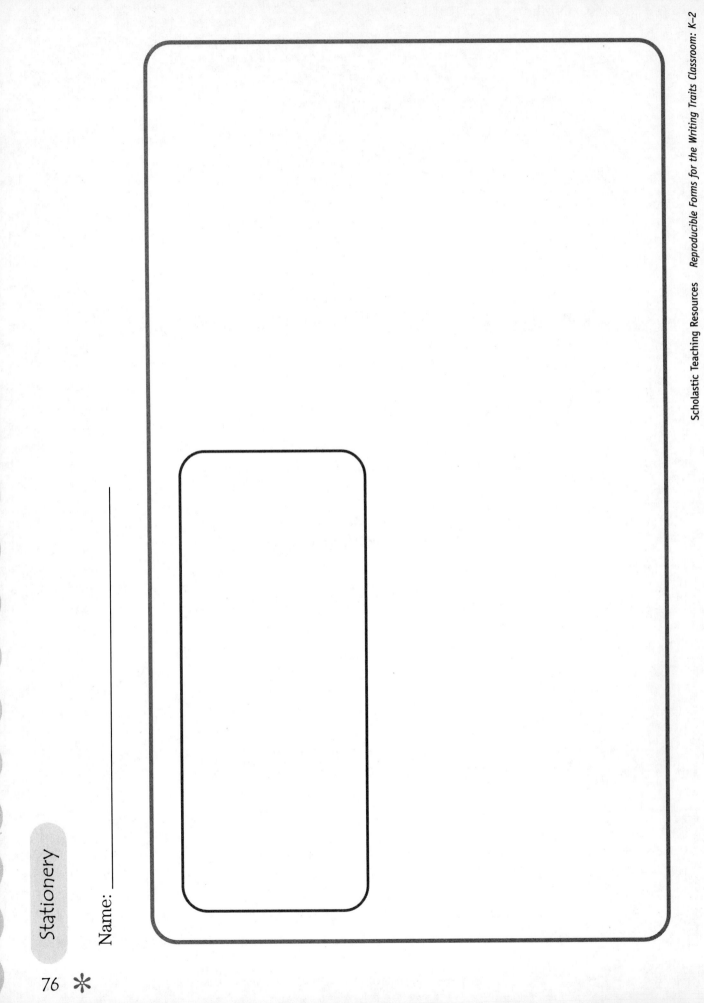

Stationery

Name: _____

Stationery

Name: _____

Stationery

Name: _____

_____

_____

_____

_____

Notes